PRESENTED TO:

_____

ANIMAL LOVER'S NAME

_____

FROM

_____

DATE

PAWVERBS FOR KIDS

PAWVERBS
~ for Kids ~

30 Heartwarming Stories about Boys, Girls, and Their Pets

JENNIFER MARSHALL BLEAKLEY

Tyndale House Publishers

CAROL STREAM, ILLINOIS

Visit Tyndale's website for kids at tyndale.com/kids.

Tyndale is a registered trademark of Tyndale House Ministries. The Tyndale Kids logo is a trademark of Tyndale House Ministries.

Pawverbs for Kids: 30 Heartwarming Stories about Boys, Girls, and Their Pets

Designed by Ron C. Kaufmann

Published in association with Jessica Kirkland and the literary agency of Kirkland Media Management, LLC.

For information about special discounts for bulk purchases, please contact Tyndale House Publishers at csresponse@tyndale.com, or call 1-855-277-9400.

Library of Congress Cataloging-in-Publication Data

A catalog record for this book is available from the Library of Congress.

ISBN 978-1-4964-6147-6

Printed in China

29 28 27 26 25 24 23
7   6   5   4   3   2   1

For Andrew and Ella:
I love you forever times infinity.

A Note from the Author

HI! MY NAME IS JEN, and I like animals—a lot. I like watching animals, playing with them, and learning about them. I think they are funny and cute and interesting. But what I love most about animals is how they help me think about and learn about God.

Did you know that animals can do that?

It's true!

If you slow down, pay attention, and ask God for help—you can learn things about *him* from the animals he created.

One of the most important things I've learned from animals is that I can talk to God as easily as I can talk to an animal.

You see, I was what you would call a shy kid. Talking to people, sometimes even to my friends, felt scary. Talking to teachers and doctors and other grown-ups was especially hard. My hands would get sweaty, and my stomach would hurt. I wanted to talk to people. I wished I could just open my mouth and talk as easily as my friends did, but it was hard, and I often felt lonely.

One day when I was sitting outside, my cat, Sugar, walked over to me and climbed onto my lap. She started purring.

"You make me feel happy and safe, Sugar," I said,

rubbing my hand back and forth on her gray-and-black fur.

I started talking to Sugar while I petted her. I told her about a hard test I had taken at school, about a friend who'd hurt my feelings, and how I wished I could try out for the school play—but that I was too scared. Sugar kept purring. She was so easy to talk to that all the words I had been holding in for a long time came out.

The next day, I went to find Sugar as soon as I got home from school. I told her that I got an okay grade on the test, made up with my friend, and signed up to be in the chorus for the school play—so I could be in the play but didn't have to try out for a speaking part. Sugar listened and purred.

The next Sunday at church, our pastor talked about the ways God cares for us. He read a verse from 1 Peter that says, "Give all your worries and cares to God, for he cares about you" (5:7). When he read that verse, I thought about Sugar and how she listened to all my worries and the things I cared about.

Later that day, while Sugar purred on my lap, I started talking to God—telling him how much I wanted to be able to talk to other people, thanking him for bringing Sugar into my life, and asking him to help me not feel so scared all the time.

That day, I realized that God was with me, like Sugar was with me—but that God was even better because he is *always* with me. Sugar couldn't go to school or to the doctor's office with me, but God could. And he did.

Sugar helped me learn that I can talk to God, and God helped me not feel as scared all the time. Sometimes I still get a little scared when I have to talk to someone new, but now I know I can talk to God about that—and he will help me.

And that's why I wrote this book. I wrote it so I would remember all the things I've learned, and I wrote it so that *you* can learn things from animals too—things about yourself, about other people, and about God.

Each story in this book is based on something that actually happened with a real animal. There is a Paws and Ponder section after each story with questions to answer so you can learn your own lessons from the animals. And there is a Paws and Pray section with a short prayer too.

You can read one story at a time or read lots of stories at once. You can read the book at bedtime or in the morning or in the afternoon. You can read the stories with your family, with a friend, by yourself, or to your pet. However you decide to read this book, I hope you will enjoy the stories and get to know God a little better through them.

Most of all, I hope you will come to know that God made you and loves you, and he thinks that you are very, very special—just the way you are.

And I think you're pretty PAWsome too!

Love, Jen

Little Autumn

Trust in the LORD with all your heart; do not depend
on your own understanding. Seek his will in all you
do, and he will show you which path to take.

PROVERBS 3:5-6

IT WAS A PERFECT DAY to be outside. The air
was cool, the sun was bright, and autumn leaves fell
like giant orange, red, and yellow raindrops.

Lizzie's dad was cleaning out the garage, and she
was raking leaves into a pile big enough for them both
to jump in. Her dad had just pulled a big box out to
the driveway when he bent down to look at something.
Lizzie ran over to see what it was.

A baby squirrel!

It was the smallest and cutest little squirrel Lizzie
had ever seen. And it was trying to climb up her dad's
pant leg!

"Maybe she thinks your leg is a tree trunk," Lizzie giggled.

The little squirrel stopped moving and looked up at Lizzie's dad.

"She must have fallen out of her nest," he said.

"What do we do?" Lizzie asked, bending down to look at the squirrel.

Her dad did a search on his phone.

"It says to leave the little squirrel near the tree where we found her, and the mother squirrel should come back soon to get her baby."

Lizzie and her dad made a temporary nest for the squirrel out of a shallow box, an old towel, and some leaves, and set it under the trees by the driveway. But hours later, the baby squirrel was still there and the air was getting cold. Lizzie's dad called the wildlife rescue phone number. They said to keep the squirrel warm overnight and then drop her off with one of their volunteers in the morning.

Lizzie looked at the little squirrel. She was so cute.

"Why don't we keep her?" Lizzie asked. "She could be our pet! We could name her Autumn since we found her in the fall!"

But her dad shook his head. "She belongs in the wild. She wouldn't be happy as a pet, and we don't know how to take care of her. As hard as it is, we need to do what is best for her—not what feels good for us."

9

Lizzie knew her dad was right, but she still wished she could keep the baby squirrel. That night, Lizzie peeked into the box. Little Autumn was curled up in a ball, sound asleep.

"You were smart to go to my dad for help. He's going to make sure you get to climb all the tallest trees and eat all the acorns and nuts you can. But I still wish I could keep you."

Several months later, Lizzie's dad got a text from the wildlife rescue volunteer with a picture of a much bigger Autumn being released into a nearby park. Seeing Autumn again—and seeing her so big and healthy looking—made Lizzie happy.

"Thanks for knowing how to take care of Autumn," she said to her dad, giving him a hug. "She was smart to trust you."

Would you have wanted to keep little Autumn? Why or why not?

Why did Lizzie's dad want to take Autumn to a wildlife rescue volunteer?

Can you think of a time when doing the right thing was hard?

Proverbs 3:5 tells us to trust God. What do you need to trust God with today?

Paws and Pray

Dear God, please help me to trust you with my whole heart. There is so much I don't understand and so much I don't know. But you know everything—and you know me and love me. Help me to trust you more and more each day.

Amelia's Gift

Honor the LORD with your wealth and with the
best part of everything you produce.

PROVERBS 3:9

AMELIA LOVES BUYING TOYS for her yellow
Lab, Ollie. Any time she gets money for her birthday
or Christmas, she uses some of it to buy Ollie a stuffed
animal or a chew toy.

She likes how Ollie jumps up and down while he
waits for his present. She likes how he wags his tail
super fast when she hands him his new toy. And she
loves all the happy little noises he makes when he
plays with it.

But most of all, Amelia likes how Ollie tries to share
his new toys with her. After playing with a new toy for
a few minutes, Ollie will bring it back to Amelia so they
can play catch.

When Amelia gets home from school, Ollie always runs to her with his newest toy in his mouth so they can play together. And when Amelia snuggles into bed at night, Ollie drops his toy on her bed.

"That toy is for you, Ollie," Amelia says, handing the toy back to him. "But thank you for sharing it with me."

A few days before Christmas, Amelia wrapped three toys for Ollie—a hedgehog stuffed animal, a giant tennis ball, and a chew bone. She couldn't wait to watch Ollie tear into the wrapping paper to get his toys.

But during the Christmas Eve service at church, Amelia listened to people talk about the gift God gave to the world when he sent his son, Jesus. She started to wonder if there was a gift she could give *God*.

Amelia loved giving gifts to Ollie—and her family—but she had never thought about giving a gift to God. And since Christmas is the day we celebrate Jesus' birthday, it seemed like a good day to give him a gift.

But what could she give Jesus?

What kind of present would he want? She thought about it that night and the next morning. But she still couldn't think of anything.

As soon as she went downstairs and saw all the presents under the tree, Amelia forgot about her question. She started opening her gifts and helping Ollie open his.

Later that day, after Amelia played fetch with Ollie, she sat down with the new paint set she had gotten from her parents. She couldn't wait to paint a picture on her new easel.

But what should she paint first?

Suddenly, Amelia knew just what to give Jesus. She would give him the first painting from her new easel.

Amelia painted a picture of a Christmas tree with lots of presents under it. And on the biggest present she wrote,

To Jesus,
    Thank you.
    Love, Amelia

What is a favorite gift you've received? Why was that
  gift so special?
What are some of the gifts God has given you?
Why is Jesus the greatest gift God has given us?
What kind of gift could you give to Jesus today?

Paws and Pray

*Dear God, thank you for all the gifts you have given me.
Thank you for the sunshine and the raindrops. Thank you
for people who care about me. Thank you for loving me.
And thank you for Jesus. Please show me what I can give
you today to say thank you for all you have done for me.*

A New Friend

Blessed is the one who finds wisdom, and
the one who gets understanding.

PROVERBS 3:13, ESV

"DEAR GOD, please help me make a new friend this year," Bethany prayed the night before starting a new school year.

It was a prayer she had prayed almost every night since her best friend, Jessa, started going to a different school. Bethany missed Jessa so much, and she worried she would feel lonely at school without her.

And she did.

She felt lonely without Jessa there to make her laugh.

She felt lonely in the cafeteria without her best friend to talk to.

And she felt lonely in the car line while she waited by herself for her mom.

"What's wrong?" Bethany's mom asked when she picked her up from school the first day.

"Nothing," Bethany answered—but the truth was, everything felt wrong.

Bethany went to bed that night feeling mad. She was mad at the kids at school for not trying harder to be her friend, she was mad at Jessa for changing schools, and she was even mad at God for not answering her prayer.

A few days later, Bethany went to her first horse-riding lesson. The lessons were a birthday gift from her mom. She was so excited to meet all the different horses. And while she liked each one she met, her favorite was a dark-brown horse named Petey. He had a white dot on his forehead, little patches of white on his feet, and gentle-looking eyes.

Bethany's lesson started with learning how to groom Petey. The instructor showed her how to brush his coat and mane, how to clean his hooves, and how to put fly spray on his legs. She didn't ride him that first day, but she didn't mind. She just liked getting to spend time with him.

At her next lesson, after another hard week of school without Jessa, Bethany found out that Petey had a sore on his back from a horsefly bite. Bethany's instructor told her that she could choose a different horse to ride. But Bethany didn't want a different horse.

"It's okay," she said, "Can I just groom Petey again?"

The instructor helped her get the grooming bucket and tie Petey's lead rope to a hook. Then she went to teach a new student how to groom a horse.

Bethany talked softly to Petey while she brushed him. She told him all about Jessa moving, how lonely she felt, and how hard it was to make new friends.

The next week, Petey's back was healed, and Bethany was able to ride him. She liked sitting up so high. Petey's back was strong, and Bethany knew she could trust him to hold her up.

"You might not be able to sit with me in the cafeteria at lunch," Bethany whispered, leaning down toward Petey's neck, "but it looks like God *did* answer my prayer for a new friend this year after all. He gave me you."

How did God answer Bethany's prayer for a friend?
Can you think of a time when God answered your
prayer in a different way than you thought he
would?
How did he answer?

*Dear God, thank you for hearing me when I talk to you
in prayer. You see everything and you know everything.
Help me trust you to answer my prayers in the way you
know is best.*

24

Snow Bath

The LORD will be at your side and will
keep your foot from being snared.

PROVERBS 3:26, NIV

GRACIE, a four-year-old golden retriever, likes going on trips with her family and exploring new places. She especially likes visiting places where there is snow.

Gracie loves snow! She likes to run in snow and dig in snow—and she really likes to eat snow.

Once when Gracie's family took a trip to the mountains, her human mom took her for a walk in the snow while the rest of their family went skiing.

Crunch, crunch, crunch.

Gracie loved the sound her paws made in the snow. She jumped, she dug, she ran in happy little circles. But all of a sudden, Gracie stopped. Her tail dropped, and her ears stood up.

What was that scary sound?

She ran to her mom's side and whined.

"It's okay, girl. Those are just the snow machines. They make snow," her mom explained.

Gracie didn't like the machines. They were too tall and too loud, and they looked like giant hoses. Gracie didn't like hoses either. They made her think of getting a bath. And she really, really didn't like getting a bath.

Gracie's mom told her that the snow machines were good because they made lots of snow for the skiers and snowboarders. But Gracie thought they were too close to the sidewalks. She was really scared.

"It's okay, Gracie," her mom said, giving her leash a gentle tug. "They won't hurt you."

Gracie trusted her mom, but she was still scared. *What if the big machine turns toward me and the giant hose tries to give me an icy bath?* Gracie's back legs started to shake.

Gracie felt her mom's hand on her back. "Look."

Gracie knew that word meant she should turn to meet her mom's eyes. So she did.

Her mom smiled and said, "Walk."

Gracie took two steps, but she got scared again when she saw the big snow machine.

"Gracie, look," her mom said again.

Gracie scooted closer to her mom. She took a big breath and started walking—fast. She walked so fast

that her mom had to run to keep up. But Gracie made it! The big snow machine didn't give her a bath.

Gracie and her mom walked toward a busy area with lots of skiers, shops, and restaurants. Gracie liked seeing all the people. She liked smelling new smells and getting petted by lots of new friends. But she still didn't like the snow machines.

On the way back to their condo, Gracie kept her eyes on her mom and walked really fast by the big machines.

Every time they walked past the machines during their vacation, Gracie stayed close to her mom. It helped to know that she was there and that she would protect Gracie from the scary snow machines.

PAWS AND PONDER

Why was Gracie scared of the snow machines?

What did her mom tell her to do?

Why did Gracie feel better knowing her mom was beside her?

How does it make you feel to know God is close to you?

Paws and Pray

Dear God, please help me to remember that you are always with me, even when I feel scared. Help me to look to you by reading the Bible, praying, and thinking about you. And please help me talk to others about you, so they will know you are with them too.

Will You Be My Friend?

Do not withhold good from those who deserve
it when it's in your power to help them.

PROVERBS 3:27

BELLE, A GRAY, BLACK, and white cat, was used
to being by herself. She lived on a farm with a human
family and was happy being their outside cat. She
spent her days chasing mice and snakes, climbing trees
and fences, and taking naps in the sun.

Belle was a happy cat who had everything she
needed. Or so she thought.

One day, after living on the farm for many years,
Belle heard a strange noise coming from the barn. Her
human family was standing around a big box. Belle
crept closer to the box to get a better look. There were
three tiny cats inside.

"Aren't they cute?" Belle heard her human sister
Adiba say. "I'm going to keep them in the barn for

now, and when they are bigger, they can roam the farm like Belle."

Belle felt a little scared of the three strange cats in the box. She walked away from the barn and hid under the porch. When Adiba called for her later that day, she didn't come out.

A few weeks later, Adiba let the little cats out to explore the farm. Belle hid behind her favorite tree to watch them. She learned that their names were Simba, Timon, and Nala.

Belle watched them pounce on pine cones, chase leaves, and play-wrestle each other. But when the one named Simba started to walk over to Belle, she got mad and hissed at him.

"Be nice, Belle," Adiba said, picking up Simba. "The kitties just want to be friends."

Belle didn't want to be friends. She liked her farm the way it was—the way it used to be. She didn't like that things had changed. Belle decided to stay far away from the barn and pretend the new cats weren't there.

But one day, while Belle was watching the three cats play together in a big haystack, she started to wish she could join them. They looked like they were having a lot of fun. Maybe she did want to be friends.

But would they want to be friends with her?

Belle walked toward the barn. As she got closer,

Simba gave a warning meow. He wasn't sure what Belle wanted, and he looked ready to fight.

Belle meowed softly, then lay down beside a wheelbarrow. She wanted the other cats to know she wasn't there to fight. She was there to make friends.

One by one, Simba, Timon, and Nala walked toward Belle.

Would they be mean? Would they meow and scratch and fight?

No. Simba, Timon, and Nala sat close to Belle and purred. They were glad she had come. They were happy to be her friends, and the four cats have been friends ever since.

Why do you think Belle was scared to be friends with the new cats?

What might have happened if Simba tried to fight with Belle?

What is something you can do to be a friend to someone this week?

Paws and Pray

Dear God, thank you for always being here to help me. Please show me how to do good to others, and help me be a friend to someone today.

Good Neighbors

Don't plot harm against your neighbor, for
those who live nearby trust you.

PROVERBS 3:29

EVERY DAY WHEN TREVOR and his older
brother, Tyler, get off the school bus, their little dog,
Jack, stands inside their fence and barks. He loves to
play fetch and can't wait for the brothers to come in
the gate and throw a ball for him.

One day when Trevor and Tyler got home, Jack
dropped a ball at Tyler's feet and started spinning
around them in tight circles.

"Okay, okay, Jack," Tyler laughed. "Go get it!"

Tyler threw the ball as far as he could. It landed in a
pile of dried leaves. Jack chased after the ball and dove
into the leaf pile to get it. He ran back and dropped the
ball at Tyler's feet. Tyler threw it again.

"Hey, I want to throw it!" Trevor whined.

"Go find your own ball," Tyler said.

Sometimes Tyler made Trevor really mad. Trevor stomped around the yard, angry that his brother had gotten the ball first. There were usually tennis balls everywhere. Why couldn't he find one today?

He finally spied a fuzzy green ball under the deck. He squatted down to get it, but as he went to grab the ball, he noticed some other things under there. A lot of other things. Trevor spotted a soccer ball, gardening gloves, a shovel—the kind you use in a sandbox—and a little kid's tennis shoe.

What are those doing under here? he wondered.

Trevor brought everything out from under the deck. Tyler threw the tennis ball for Jack and then walked over to see what Trevor had found.

"Hey, that's a nice soccer ball. Why was it under the deck?"

Trevor shrugged. "I don't know."

Trevor threw the tennis ball he'd just found for Jack. As the brown-and-white dog chased after his ball, their four-year-old neighbor, Bennett, called out from the fence between their houses, "Hey! Dat's my ball!"

The little boy was pointing at the soccer ball Tyler was holding.

"Are these yours too?" Trevor asked, holding up the gloves, shovel, and shoe.

Bennett nodded, then asked, "Why you take my stuff?"

Trevor and Tyler looked at each other. They hadn't taken Bennett's things. Trevor was about to say he didn't know who had taken them, when Jack came running over.

Bennett reached his arm through the wood slats. "Hi, doggie! Come, doggie!"

Trevor looked along the fence and spotted a Jack-sized hole near the corner. He showed Tyler.

"Jack!" Tyler called out. "Have you been stealing Bennett's toys?"

Jack grabbed his tennis ball and ran to the deck.

"I'm telling Mom!" Trevor shouted, laughing at his guilty-looking dog.

"Sorry, Bennett," Tyler said. "Our dad will fix the hole so Jack can't steal your toys anymore."

Tyler and Trevor's dad did fix the hole. But every once in a while, one of Bennett's toys will appear under the deck, and their dad has to fill in another Jack-sized gap.

Thankfully, Bennett doesn't seem to mind Jack taking his toys—as long as Tyler and Trevor give them back.

PAWS AND PONDER

What does it mean to be a good neighbor?

Why didn't Jack act like a very good neighbor to Bennett?

What are some things you could do to show kindness and God's love to one of your neighbors this week?

Paws and Pray

Dear God, please help me be a good neighbor and a good friend to those around me. Help me show your love and kindness to someone today, and help me treat others like I want them to treat me.

Copper the Hero

Don't turn your back on wisdom, for she will protect you. Love her, and she will guard you.

PROVERBS 4:6

KEYSHA WAS SO EXCITED to explore the woods around the cabin her parents had rented for a week. She climbed a giant rock, crawled across a fallen tree, and found an owl feather.

When she ran back to the cabin to show her parents what she had found, a reddish-brown dog was lying by her dad's feet.

"He was here when I came outside to check on you," her dad said. "He doesn't have a collar or tag, but he looks well taken care of. He must live around here somewhere and just came over to say hi."

Keysha knelt down and petted the dog's copper-colored coat.

"I'll call him Copper," she said, wishing he could be her dog.

Keysha went inside to get Copper a bowl of water and a piece of bread. The dog ate the bread in one gulp and drank all the water. Keysha petted him for a while. Then Copper stood up, walked down the porch steps, and disappeared into the woods.

Keysha was sad that he'd left—but happy he had come.

The next morning, as Keysha and her family left for a hike to a waterfall, Copper was at the back door! Keysha was happy when Copper started following them.

"He will probably get tired soon and go home," her mom said.

But he never did.

Instead, he followed them all the way to the waterfall. He took a long drink from the creek and ate the crust from Keysha's sandwich when they stopped for a picnic.

While her mom and dad rested, Keysha and Copper explored the woods around the waterfall. Keysha had just picked up a big acorn when Copper started to bark—a low, deep bark. Keysha tried to get around Copper to go back to her parents. But he wouldn't let her pass. He kept barking and looking at something in front of her.

Keysha started to get scared.

"Dad!" she called out.

When her father got close to Copper, he put his hands up and said, "Keysha, don't move."

There was a venomous snake on the path, camouflaged in all the leaves. Her dad grabbed a long stick and shooed the snake away.

"It was a good thing we had Copper with us today, or you might have stepped on the snake," her dad said, patting the dog on the back.

When they returned to the cabin, Keysha's mom cooked Copper his very own hamburger. And for the rest of their trip, Keysha would only play outside if Copper was with her.

"Thanks for being here, Copper," she said on their last day. "And thanks for protecting me. I'll never forget you."

And she never, ever did.

How did Copper protect Keysha?

What might have happened if Copper hadn't been there, or if Keysha hadn't paid attention to his warning?

What is wisdom? How can it protect us?

Paws and Pray

Dear God, thank you for all the ways you protect me. Please help me listen to the wise people you have put in my life. And please help me grow to become a wise person who listens to you and protects others.

Gypsy's Treasures

Take hold of my instructions; don't let them go.
Guard them, for they are the key to life.

PROVERBS 4:13

"**MOM!**" Landon called out. "Where are my baseball socks?"

"I don't know, Landon," his mom called back. "But hurry up. We have to go."

Landon knew he had left his socks on his dresser. He'd set them there the night before so he wouldn't forget them. They were the socks he always wore to a big game. He frowned as he grabbed his second-favorite pair of socks from the drawer.

"Bye, Gypsy," he called out to his chocolate-colored dog, who was curled up on the rug beside his bed.

The next day, Landon's brother, Ryland, couldn't find his goggles.

"Mom! I need my goggles for swim practice," he grumbled. "I know they were in my swim bag."

Gypsy was sleeping on her bed, but she raised her head to watch Ryland search. He picked up his bag from where he had dropped it the day before. He found his towel, his shower shoes, and his swim cap. But no goggles. He had to borrow Landon's old ones.

A few days later, when Landon and Ryland's mom was pulling weeds, she lost her gardening gloves. She had laid them in the grass when she went inside to get a drink of water. But when she came back, they were gone.

"They were right here," she said.

Landon and Ryland were outside playing baseball. They came over to help their mom find her gloves. Landon looked in the bushes. Ryland looked under a big rock. And their mom checked the trash can. No gloves.

Gypsy was lying in a patch of dirt, watching her family search. Landon turned his head to the side and looked a little closer. Something was poking out from under Gypsy.

Landon walked closer to his dog. She laid her head down and wouldn't look at him.

"Gypsy, did you take Mom's gloves?"

When Landon knelt down, he saw the purple finger

of a glove poking out from the dirt under her belly. But that wasn't all.

Buried under loose soil and leaves were Landon's baseball socks, Ryland's goggles, their dad's favorite T-shirt, and two empty juice boxes.

"So you're the one who's been taking our things!" Landon's mom said, laughing. "I guess you decided that if this stuff was important to us, it was important to you, huh?"

From then on, every time something went missing, they knew to look for Gypsy—who usually had it, and who guarded it well.

PAWS AND PONDER

What are some of your favorite things?
Why are they important to you?
Proverbs 4:13 tells us to take hold of and guard God's
   instructions. What does it mean to do that?

Paws and Pray

Dear God, thank you for giving us your instructions in the Bible. Help me to understand your Word and to learn how to take hold of and guard your instructions.

Mercy Is My Courage

I have counsel and sound wisdom;
I have insight; I have strength.

PROVERBS 8:14, ESV

SAM LIKES MAKING ART. He likes drawing, painting, and making things with clay. But when his grandma told him she signed him up for an art class, Sam got mad. His insides felt fuzzy, his head felt hot, and his voice got loud.

"I don't want to go to art class!" he shouted.

Sam felt bad about yelling, but he really didn't want to go. A new class would be too scary, and sometimes feeling scared makes Sam angry. He wished he could be brave. But recently, it felt like all his courage had gone away.

A few days later, his grandma took him to a place called HopeWell Ranch, where people dealing with hard things can go and spend time with horses. Sam

felt a little scared, but his grandma said she would stay with him.

A nice lady named Jodi took Sam and his grandma into a big field where horses were eating grass.

"Would you like to take one of our horses into the arena over there?" Jodi asked, pointing to a big building nearby.

Sam felt scared, but he really wanted to say yes. He chewed on his lip and nodded.

A few minutes later, a big black horse with a white stripe on her face started walking toward him. The horse was really big, but for some reason Sam didn't feel scared anymore.

"This is Mercy," Jodi said. "And I think she is asking if she can go to the arena with you. Is that okay?"

Sam nodded again.

Jodi put a halter over Mercy's head and let Sam hold the lead rope while they walked Mercy into the big building.

Sam liked Mercy.

She was big, but gentle.

Strong, but slow.

Sam learned how to brush her back and her mane. He learned how to clean her feet, and he even got to sit on her back. Sam felt brave on Mercy's back. It was like she was giving him her strength.

Sam was sad when his visit was over, but he was happy when he got to visit Mercy again the next week. And the next. And after a couple of weeks, he didn't even need his grandma to stay with him anymore.

Sam enjoyed being with Mercy. She didn't rush him. She listened when he talked. She was quiet when he was quiet. And she wasn't scared of his big feelings. Being with Mercy helped Sam learn how to deal with those feelings by talking about them, praying about them, and sometimes even drawing pictures of them.

After his fourth visit with Mercy, Sam ran up to his grandma and said, "I'm ready to start art class now."

"You are?" she asked. She sounded surprised and happy. "What changed?"

"I found my courage," Sam said, pointing to the horse. "Mercy is my courage. She helps me remember that I can be brave."

Sam was very brave when he went to the new art class. He liked it a lot. And the first picture he drew was of Mercy.

Why did Sam feel scared and angry?

What did Sam learn from Mercy?

Where do you find your courage?

What do you need to ask God to help you do today?

Paws and Pray

Dear God, thank you for being my strength and my courage. Please help me remember that I can always talk to you about my feelings. And please help me learn more about you so I can be wise.

Moe, Listen

Listen to my instruction and be wise. Don't ignore it.

PROVERBS 8:33

ABBY COULDN'T STOP staring at the big brown dog at the park. She had never seen a dog with no eyes before.

"Mama, that dog doesn't have any eyes!" Abby called out, pointing to the dog.

The dog's owner smiled, but Abby's mom did not. She told Abby to be quiet and eat her picnic lunch. But Abby didn't want to eat her lunch. She wanted to see the dog. So while Abby's mom cut the crust off her little brother's sandwich, Abby followed the dog and his owner to the edge of the lake.

"Okay, Moe," the woman said to her dog. "Listen."

Abby squeezed her eyes shut and listened too. She heard a *ploop* sound. Something hit the water.

"Moe, get your ball," the woman said.

When Abby opened her eyes, Moe was running into the lake—straight to his ball. He dipped his head into the water and scooped the ball into his mouth. Abby clapped.

Moe ran back to the lady. She petted him and told him that he did a good job.

Abby closed her eyes again.

It must be hard to find a little ball in a big lake when you can't see, she thought.

"Moe, listen," the lady said before throwing the ball.

Abby clapped for Moe when he fetched his ball again. Abby's eyes got big when Moe's owner said, "Moe, come. Left side," and the dog walked over to her left side and sat down.

Moe was such a good listener that he didn't even need his eyes. As long as he listened to the lady, he knew just where to go.

"Abby!" her mom called from the picnic table.

Uh-oh.

Now it was time for Abby to be a good listener.

"Coming, Mama!"

Why was it important for Moe to listen to his owner?
What could have happened if Abby didn't listen to
    her mom when she called?
How can listening make us wise?

Paws and Pray

*Dear God, I want to be wise. Please help me listen to you
and to the wise people you've put in my life. Help me to
obey you, even when it's hard.*

Slow Down, Champ

You are the one who will profit if you have wisdom,
and if you reject it, you are the one who will suffer.

PROVERBS 9:12, GNT

DAVIS WAS SO EXCITED to finally be at his aunt and uncle's farm. He and his family had been driving for five hours, and their one-year-old hound dog, Champ, had been panting loudly and making a lot of stinky smells. When Davis's dad stopped the car, Davis threw open the door and ran out of the car. So did Champ.

Champ had never been to the farm before. He was used to their small backyard at home, and he seemed confused by the hundred acres of land they were on. Davis's aunt and uncle had ponds for fishing, hills for dirt-bike riding, mud puddles for ATV riding, open space for playing games, and lots and lots of trails for walking. Davis loved visiting the farm every

summer—and he especially liked playing with his cousins. They were a few years older than Davis, but they were always really nice to him.

Champ sniffed Davis's cousins and his aunt and uncle—and then he started running. He ran to the pond. He ran *into* the pond. He ran up the hills and down the hills. He ran circles in the open field, zigzags in the woods, and a straight line into the mud.

"Oh, Champ," Davis heard his mom say. "You're going to have to slow down."

But Champ didn't listen.

After rolling in the mud, Champ chased a squirrel up a tree, chased a bunny into a bush, and then ran more zigzags in the woods. Davis's dad tried to catch him to make him slow down, but Champ zoomed away from him.

"He's going to hurt himself," Davis's mom worried.

At dinner that night, Davis noticed Champ was limping. He had run so hard and for so long that he had gotten sores on his paws. Champ had to spend the next three days in a dog crate so his paws could heal.

"You should have listened to Mom," Davis said when he brought Champ a treat.

The day before Davis's family had to leave, Champ's paws were healed enough that he was allowed to play. At first, it looked like the dog had learned his lesson. He only ran around for a few minutes before lying in the grass to watch a large bird on the pond. But when the bird flew away, Champ jumped up, barked, and started running. And never stopped.

"Oh, Champ, when will you learn?" Davis said, shaking his head.

The ride back home was much quieter with Champ sound asleep in the back seat. In fact, Champ slept the whole way home. But with the way his paws were moving, it looked like the dog was still running in his dreams.

PAWS AND PONDER

Why didn't Champ want to slow down?
Why is it important to listen to people who are wise?
Where do we find wisdom?

Paws and Pray

Dear God, I want to be wise. Please help me learn from wise people and from the wisdom of the Bible. Help me to make wise choices, even when it's hard.

Hungry Squirrels

Laziness leads to poverty; hard work makes you rich.

PROVERBS 10:4, CEV

MICAH LIKED WATCHING squirrels try to climb up the bird feeders in his backyard. He thought it was funny to watch them jump from the trees, swing on the feeders, and hang upside down while they ate the birdseed. But his mom did not like it, and every time she saw a squirrel on the feeder, she ran outside to chase it away.

"They're just hungry," Micah said.

"Our yard is full of acorns and other things for them to eat," his mom answered. "I paid a lot of money for those bird feeders, and I don't want the squirrels to break them."

Day after day, Micah watched squirrels try to get to the bird feeders, only to be chased away by his mom or their dog, Buster. Micah tried to help the squirrels by

picking up acorns from their yard and leaving them on the deck rail. But Buster usually pushed them off—or tried to eat them himself.

One day, when Micah went to Home Depot with his mom to get a new bird feeder, he saw a sign about a workshop that started in five minutes where kids could make a birdhouse to take home. Micah's mom walked him to the workshop area, where three long tables were set up with supplies. She said she would be back in twenty minutes to get him. A man wearing an orange work apron with tools in the pockets asked what kind of birdhouse Micah wanted to make.

"I don't want to make a birdhouse," Micah answered. "I want to make a squirrel feeder, because squirrels get hungry too."

"What a great idea," the man said.

He helped Micah make a tray-style feeder that could hang from a tree. He showed Micah how to nail four small boards together to form an open square. He helped him nail a flat sheet of wood to the bottom. And he helped Micah use a drill to make holes in two of the boards to put wire through so he could hang the feeder on a tree branch.

Micah was excited to show his mom.

"I love it, Micah!" she said.

Micah hung the squirrel feeder in a tree as soon as they got home. He filled it with squirrel food his mom had bought and with some acorns from the yard.

The next morning, Micah saw two squirrels sitting in their feeder and one waiting on the branch for a turn.

Micah was happy and proud that the squirrels were enjoying his hard work—and his mom was happy that the squirrels weren't on her bird feeders.

How did Micah's hard work help the squirrels?
Can you think of a time when you worked hard to
    help someone else?
When has someone worked hard to help you?

Paws and Pray

Dear God, thank you for all you do to help me. Please help me be willing to work hard for others and to obey you.

I'll Love You Forever

Hatred stirs up conflict, but love covers over all wrongs.

PROVERBS 10:12, NIV

A BROWN-AND-WHITE dog limped toward the fence where his two dog friends lived. He had crawled under the fence many times before to play with Daman and Dante, but this time he yelped in pain. His shoulder hurt. It was bleeding.

Daman and Dante started barking. The brown-and-white dog wanted to play, but he felt so tired. A lady came outside.

"Oh my goodness! Someone hurt that dog!" the lady yelled, running back in the house.

The brown-and-white dog was scared. The last human he had gotten close to had hurt him. *What if this human hurts me too?* The dog crawled back under the fence and hid in some bushes. He heard the lady call for him, but he was too scared to move.

The next day when he crawled out from the bushes, he found bowls of food and water. The brown-and-white dog ate and drank as fast as he could. As he was finishing the last bite of food, he heard his dog friends bark. They were close. And so was the lady. The dog wanted to run, but his shoulder hurt, and he was tired. The lady walked over to him. He closed his eyes and waited for more pain. But the lady just put a leash on him.

"Come on, little one. Let's get you some help," she said.

The lady put him in her car and drove him to an animal hospital. A vet bandaged him up and gave him medicine to help him feel better. The brown-and-white dog went home with the nice lady, who let him sleep inside and gave him lots of food.

"When you're feeling better, we will find you a nice place to live with people who will see how special you are and take good care of you," the lady told him.

Two months later, when the brown-and-white dog's shoulder was healed, the lady took him to a place called an animal shelter. The dog was scared. *What if I get hurt again?*

All of a sudden, he heard a woman's voice. She was talking to the person who took care of him at the shelter. The woman had the nicest-sounding voice the dog

had ever heard. And when she looked at him, he felt warm inside.

"I'm Sarah," the woman said, then pointed to a man beside her. "This is my husband, Kory. We think you are the bravest, most handsome and special dog in the whole wide world. And we would like you to be our dog. What do you think?"

The brown-and-white dog felt a little scared, but he took two brave steps toward Sarah and laid his head on her hand. She felt like home.

"Good boy," Sarah whispered. "You're safe now. And I promise to love you forever and ever."

The dog looked deep into her eyes and knew that he would always love her too.

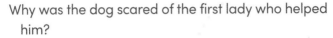

PAWS AND PONDER

Why was the dog scared of the first lady who helped him?

When has someone shown you love and kindness after you've been hurt?

How can you be loving and kind to someone today?

Paws and Pray

Dear God, thank you for always loving me. Help me to remember your love and kindness. And please help me to show your love and kindness to others.

Jumping Bean

AIDEN WAS SO HAPPY to have a puppy.

He and his parents had met lots and lots of dogs at the animal shelter, but when a volunteer brought out a little black-and-white puppy, Aiden knew that was his dog.

"He looks like a big jelly bean," Aiden said when the puppy crawled into his lap and curled up in a ball.

The name stuck. And Aiden thought Jelly Bean—who they called Bean for short—was the best dog in the world.

And he was, except for one thing—Bean jumped on everyone.

Aiden liked when Bean jumped on him every day when he got home from school. It made him happy to see his puppy so excited. But Aiden's mom and dad didn't want Bean to jump.

"He's going to be a big dog," his mom said.

"And we need to teach him not to jump on people now, so he won't hurt someone when he's bigger," his dad added.

Aiden understood what they were saying, but he thought it was fun when Bean jumped. *He can just jump on me*, Aiden thought.

Aiden's parents worked to teach Bean not to jump on them. But when they weren't looking, Aiden would let Bean jump on him.

He's just a little puppy, Aiden thought. *He won't hurt anybody.*

A few months later, Aiden's Uncle Gary, Aunt Maggie, and little cousin Haley came to visit. Bean had gotten a lot bigger since the last time they'd seen him, and Aiden was excited to play with Haley and Bean. But when Haley walked into the house, Bean jumped on her, and Haley fell down and bumped her head on the wall.

Aiden's mom got ice for Haley's head, and his dad clipped Bean's leash on so he couldn't jump on anyone else.

Haley had gotten hurt, and Bean was stuck on a leash time-out. *This is all my fault*, Aiden thought. He felt like crying, but he didn't want anyone to see, so he went upstairs to hide in his closet.

"Knock, knock," his dad called out a few minutes later.

Aiden opened the closet door. He couldn't hide his tears anymore.

"I'm sorry that Haley got hurt. It's all my fault."

Aiden's dad gave him a hug. "Bean is still a puppy, which means he's still learning his manners," his dad said. "And we could really use your help to teach him how to behave around people. Will you help us?"

Aiden promised he would.

And he kept his promise. He helped Bean learn to keep all four paws on the ground when he greeted people. And now when Haley comes to visit, she loves playing with Bean—who knows to be gentle around her. And that makes Aiden very happy.

Why didn't Aiden want to obey his parents at first?
What made him change his mind?

Why was Aiden able to keep his promise to his dad after Haley got hurt?

What do you think Aiden learned?

Paws and Pray

Dear God, sometimes it's really hard not to get my own way. Please help me to obey you. And help me do my best to obey my parents, teachers, and the other leaders in my life. Thank you for forgiving me when I mess up. And please help me to forgive other people too.

Praying for a Cat

The hopes of the godly result in happiness, but the expectations of the wicked come to nothing.

PROVERBS 10:28

MATEO AND HIS LITTLE SISTER, Ana, loved playing with their friend's cat. One day, they asked their mom if they could get a cat of their own.

"I'm sorry, guys," she said with a frown, "but I'm allergic to cats. I would get sick if we had a cat in our house."

Mateo didn't want his mom to get sick. But he really wanted a cat.

"What if we got a cat that lived outside?" he asked.

His mom thought for a few minutes.

"If we ever find a stray cat who needs someone to take care of it, then we could keep it—outside," she said.

Mateo hugged his mom and ran off to tell his sister.

They decided to start praying, asking God to send them a cat.

Every night for two weeks, they prayed for a cat.

But no cat came.

Mateo felt sad. He thought for sure God was going to answer his prayer and send them a cat. The next week he went to summer camp and forgot to pray about a cat. When he got home, he started praying again, but only every other night or so.

Still no cat.

Months passed. Mateo started to think that maybe God hadn't heard his prayers. Or maybe God didn't want them to have a cat. That would be hard, but Mateo knew he could trust God, even if the answer to his prayer was no.

A year later, on a warm spring day, Mateo's mom asked him to go get the mail. As Mateo was walking to the end of the driveway, he saw a cat dart into the bushes beside the mailbox.

Meow!

"Oh wow! A cat! Stay here!" Mateo said, hoping the cat would listen.

He ran to the house and burst through the back door.

"I found a cat!" he yelled. "I need some—some—" *What would a cat want to eat?* "I need some turkey and some water!"

Ana jumped off her chair, squealed, and ran to the refrigerator. She grabbed a package of turkey while Mateo filled a plastic bowl with water. The two of them ran to the mailbox, while their mom followed.

Mateo put the bowl beside the bush and held out a slice of turkey.

A very skinny gray-and-black cat with the bushiest tail Mateo had ever seen crept slowly toward them.

"Poor thing looks like he's been on his own for a while," his mom said.

The cat stopped in front of Mateo and meowed. Mateo laid the turkey in the grass and waited. The cat ate the turkey, then rubbed his head on Mateo's leg.

"You finally found us," he said, reaching out to touch the cat.

And when no one in their neighborhood answered their signs or emails about a lost cat, Mateo's mom said that they could keep him, as long as he lived outside.

Mateo had learned that God always hears our prayers. And even if God doesn't answer in the way we wish he would (or as fast as we wish he would), Mateo learned that he can always trust God to do what's best.

PAWS AND PONDER

Why did Mateo think God hadn't heard his prayers?

Have you ever prayed for something and felt like God didn't answer your prayer? How did that make you feel?

What do you think Mateo learned about trusting God?

Paws and Pray

Dear God, thank you for always hearing me when I talk to you, even if I don't get what I ask for. Help me to remember that you love me and that you always want what is best for me. Help me to be patient and to trust you when I pray.

A Sweet Melody

No one who gossips can be trusted with a secret, but you can put confidence in someone who is trustworthy.

PROVERBS 11:13, GNT

ISABELLA HAD NEVER felt so embarrassed. Her best friend, Cora, told everyone at their lunch table that Isabella liked Noah. Cora said she was sorry. She said she forgot it was supposed to be a secret. But now all their friends knew—and Isabella never wanted to go back to school.

Her stepmom asked her what was wrong when she picked her up. But Isabella didn't want to talk about it. She just wanted to go home.

When they got home, Isabella ran straight to the sofa and lay on her stomach with her head smushed into a cushion. Her goldendoodle, Melody, ran into the room and pushed her wet nose against Isabella's cheek.

Isabella stuck her arm out to pet Melody. A few minutes later, she felt the cushion dip when her step-mom sat down beside her.

"You know," her stepmom said, rubbing small circles on Isabella's back, "Melody is really good at keeping secrets."

"That's because she can't talk," Isabella mumbled into the sofa cushion.

"That's what makes her such a great secret keeper. After all, she's never told you any of my secrets, has she?"

Isabella turned over to look at her stepmom. "You tell Melody secrets?"

"I sure do," her stepmom said. "Big ones too."

"Like what?" Isabella asked, sitting up a little.

"Well, one secret I've told Melody—that I'll share with you because I know I can trust you—is that I'm scared of talking in front of people."

Isabella raised her eyebrows. "But you talk in front of people all the time. It's part of your job."

Her stepmom smiled. "I know, but I'm terrified every time I do it."

"Will you tell me another secret?" Isabella asked.

Her stepmom nodded and chewed on her bottom lip. "Well, deep down in my heart, I still feel like I'm in middle school—and worried about what everyone thinks of me."

"For real?" Isabella asked.

"For real," her stepmom admitted.

"And Melody helps you feel better?"

"She really does. Melody always listens, and I never have to worry about her laughing at me or telling anybody what I said. She's a really good friend."

Isabella scooted off the sofa and sat next to Melody.

"Do you mind if I talk to Melody for a little bit?" she asked.

Her stepmom kissed the top of her head. "Talking to Melody is a great idea."

When her stepmom left the room, Isabella told Melody all about what happened at lunch and how much it had hurt her feelings. And she was surprised that she really did feel a little better.

Isabella realized that all friends mess up sometimes, but she was really glad to have a dog who would never tell her secrets—and a stepmom who understood how hard it is sometimes to be a kid.

PAWS AND PONDER

Why did Isabella feel embarrassed?

When is a time you felt embarrassed? What did you do?

Who is a trustworthy person (or animal) you can talk to?

Why is it important to be a trustworthy friend?

Paws and Pray

Dear God, I know I can talk to you about anything and you will always listen. I know I can trust you and your promises. Please help me be someone my friends can trust. And please help me find people I can trust.

Pony Splashes

Be generous, and you will be prosperous.
Help others, and you will be helped.

PROVERBS 11:25, GNT

DAKOTA WAS ONLY three years old when Brooklyn's parents brought her to their farm. Brooklyn was excited to have the black-and-white pony join them, but she worried Dakota would feel scared around the other five horses who were bigger, older, and stronger.

But Dakota wasn't scared at all.

In fact, the little pony became a brave leader for the herd.

One hot summer day, Brooklyn found Dakota standing with her front legs in the big black water trough.

"What are you doing, silly pony?" Brooklyn laughed.

Dakota started stomping her front legs. Water splashed everywhere.

Two of the largest horses on the farm, Juno and Tirzah, walked over to see what Dakota was doing. They had always been a little scared of water, so Brooklyn was surprised they were standing so close. She was even more surprised when the two older horses started kicking their front legs in the air like Dakota was kicking hers in the water.

"Are you pretending to splash too?" Brooklyn asked.

The harder Dakota splashed, the harder Juno and Tirzah kicked. After a while, Dakota stopped splashing. She pulled her legs out of the water and went off to eat some hay.

Juno crept closer to the big black water trough. She lowered her head toward the water. She bumped it with her hoof. And then she put her front leg in the trough and kicked. She took it right back out and ran to Dakota.

Brooklyn's mouth fell open when Tirzah put her leg in the water to splash too!

The little pony had helped the bigger, older horses feel brave around the water.

But days later, when the farrier came to take care of the horses' feet, it was Dakota's turn to get scared. She started neighing loudly, running fast, and breathing hard.

Thankfully, Juno and Tirzah were there to help.

They stood close to Dakota and breathed long, slow breaths, which helped her calm down. Soon Dakota was calm enough to get her hooves trimmed—which is kind of like humans getting their fingernails cut.

"Good job helping each other," Brooklyn told the horses after the farrier left.

She gave each of them an apple slice, then laughed as Dakota put her freshly trimmed hoof back into the water trough and splashed.

PAWS AND PONDER

How did Dakota, Juno, and Tirzah help each other?
What are some ways God helps you?
How can you show kindness to someone or help
  someone today?

Paws and Pray

Dear God, thank you for all the ways you help me. I want
to follow your example and be generous and help others.
Please show me someone I can help today.

Wilbur

The righteous care for the needs of their animals.

PROVERBS 12:10, NIV

CAITLIN WAS SO EXCITED to have her very own guinea pig. She had worked hard raking leaves and pulling weeds for her grandparents to earn enough money to buy one. And she had saved all the money she had gotten for her birthday and Christmas to buy all the things he would need—like a large cage, a water bottle and food bowl, a hay rack, and a toy house to hide in.

Once everything was ready, it was finally time to bring her new pet home. She named the brown-and-white guinea pig Wilbur—after the pig in *Charlotte's Web*.

Caitlin loved taking care of Wilbur. He was the perfect-sized pet for their apartment. She gave him fresh food and water every day, cleaned his cage every week, and brushed his fur often. Every Saturday, Caitlin let Wilbur out of his cage to explore and run around her room. And every Sunday, she set up a little obstacle course for him in the hallway. She would hide his favorite treats under socks and towels and behind shoes, and she would create pathways out of Legos and Lincoln Logs. She loved watching him explore and find his treats.

But when summertime came, Caitlin started spending more time at the pool with her friends and less time with Wilbur. She fed him and gave him water, but her mom had to remind her to clean his cage. And Caitlin was too busy with her friends on the weekends to set up obstacle courses for Wilbur.

When summer break was over, Caitlin was excited to see her friends at school. But two of them had moved away, and another one said she wanted to be friends with someone else. Caitlin felt sad. And alone. She went to her room when she got home, lay on her bed, and held her favorite stuffed animal. She looked up and saw Wilbur in his cage. He looked . . . alone.

"Do you feel lonely too?" she asked.

Caitlin walked over to his cage, took the lid off, and lifted him up. "I'm sorry if you feel alone. I won't let you feel that way anymore."

And she didn't. From that day on, Caitlin took excellent care of her guinea pig.

She fed him, kept his cage clean, and played with him.

She let him sit on her lap when she played video games.

When she made new friends, she brought them over to meet and play with Wilbur.

And every Sunday, she made him his very own obstacle course.

How did Caitlin and Wilbur help each other when they were both lonely?

How can you take care of the animals around you? Maybe you could fill a bird feeder with birdseed or raise money for an animal shelter. Come up with more of your own ideas!

Why do you think it is important for us to take care of animals?

Paws and Pray

Dear God, thank you for making so many different kinds of animals. And thank you for all the ways you care for your creation—including me!

Not a Scaredy-Cat

The words of the reckless pierce like swords,
but the tongue of the wise brings healing.

PROVERBS 12:18, NIV

CHLOE WORRIED ABOUT a lot of things.

Will I make the team?

What if I get a bad grade?

Do my friends really like me?

She was also scared of a lot of things—the dark, being alone, snakes, and eating zucchini.

"You're such a scaredy-cat," Chloe's brother Matt would often tease.

Chloe would laugh and pretend his words didn't hurt, but they did.

She didn't want to be a scaredy-cat. She wanted to feel brave and strong. But it seemed like the more she tried not to worry, the more she worried.

One day, Chloe went with her mom to visit a friend who lived on a farm. While Chloe's mom talked with her friend, Chloe went to see the animals. She watched the horses for a long time, but she was too scared to touch them. She liked the way the chickens pecked at the grass, but she was scared of their pointy beaks. And she thought the goats were funny, but she'd read somewhere that they could carry diseases, so she didn't get too close.

Chloe sat down at a picnic table. Normally the farm was a fun place for her to explore. But for some reason, today it made her feel like the scaredy-cat her brother said she was.

Meow.

A gray-and-black cat looked up at her.

"Oh! Hi," Chloe said.

She had always liked cats. In fact, she wished she could have one as a pet.

The cat jumped up on the bench and rubbed his head on Chloe's leg. She gently touched the cat's back and smiled when he purred. After a few minutes, the cat climbed onto her lap. At first, Chloe worried:

What if he scratches me?

Do cats bite?

What if he has fleas?

But the little cat just curled into a ball on Chloe's lap and fell asleep.

"Well, you're not so scary," Chloe said, laying her hand on the cat's back.

Chloe liked the way his fur felt—and the way his chest vibrated as he purred in his sleep. Chloe closed her eyes and took a deep breath. The sweet smell of hay tickled her nose. The soft sound of leaves rustling high up in the trees made her lift her face to the cool breeze. When she opened her eyes and looked up at the bright-blue sky, she realized that for the first time in a long time, she wasn't worried about anything.

Chloe suddenly remembered her brother's nickname for her, and she started to laugh.

"You're not a scaredy-cat, and neither am I," she whispered to the cat.

Chloe talked to the sleeping cat about the animals on the farm and about some of the things that scared her. The more she talked, the less scared she felt.

And when she left the farm that day, Chloe felt proud of herself for being so brave.

PAWS AND PONDER

What did Chloe's brother do that hurt her feelings?

What has someone said to you that hurt your feelings?

Why do you think being with the cat helped Chloe feel a little better?

Paws and Pray

Dear God, please help me speak kind words to others. And when others say mean things, please help me remember the kind words you have spoken to me in the Bible. Help your words become the most important words to me.

I'm Glad You're Here

Anxiety weighs down the heart, but a kind word cheers it up.

PROVERBS 12:25, NIV

"DO YOU REALLY have to go?" Jordyn asked her best friend, Darcy.

"Yeah." Darcy frowned. "My dad starts his new job next week."

Jordyn couldn't believe her friend was moving three states away. She and Darcy had been best friends since they could walk. And since Darcy lived right across the street from Jordyn, they didn't have to walk far to see each other.

Meow.

"I'm gonna miss you, too, DJ," Jordyn said, petting the brown-and-white cat she and Darcy had been taking care of the past two years.

Darcy's dad had found the cat living under the dumpster behind his office and brought it home—just

like he had brought home many other stray animals over the years. The cat stayed outside, and Darcy and Jordyn fed her and played with her every day after school. And since both of Jordyn's parents were allergic to cat and dog fur, Jordyn loved getting to play with the animals at Darcy's house. Sometimes she even pretended they were her pets.

But now Darcy and all of her animals were moving far away.

Jordyn gave DJ one last pet, hugged Darcy, and went back home.

The next day, Jordyn and her parents went to Darcy's house for dinner. Jordyn knew it was the last dinner they would have together before her best friend moved five hundred miles away. She had just taken a big bite of a roll when Darcy's dad cleared his throat.

"Jordyn, we have something important to ask you," he said.

"Um, okay," she mumbled, trying to speak with a mouth full of bread.

"We've been talking, and we don't think DJ is going to like being stuck in a cat carrier for two days while we drive to our new house. We're also worried she will try and run away when we get there. So we were hoping we could leave her here with you. Would that be okay?"

Jordyn smiled so big her cheeks hurt.

"Wait, are you sure?" she asked, looking at Darcy. She wanted to keep DJ more than anything, but not if it would make Darcy sad.

"We're sure," Darcy said. "DJ can be your outside cat—and besides, it won't be long before my dad finds more stray animals to bring to our new house."

Everyone laughed.

"We think it's time for you to have your very own pet," Jordyn's mom said. Then she added, "As long as she stays outside."

Jordyn jumped up and hugged Darcy.

"Thank you," she said to Darcy's dad.

Three days later, after Jordyn waved goodbye to Darcy, DJ rubbed her head against Jordyn's leg and meowed.

Jordyn sat in the grass and petted her cat. "I miss her too," she said. "But I'm so glad you're here."

Has someone you loved ever moved away? How did that make you feel?

Proverbs 12:25 says a kind word can cheer up a person's heart. What kind words cheered Jordyn's heart?

Who can you say a kind word to today?

Paws and Pray

Dear God, please help me use kind words with people. And when my heart is sad, please send people to share kind words with me. Thank you for loving me and for comforting me during hard times.

Don't Eat the Dragon

The godly give good advice to their friends;
the wicked lead them astray.

PROVERBS 12:26

TWO YEARS AGO, Michael used his birthday money to buy a bearded dragon. He named his new pet Captain Tim. Michael set up a big glass tank that would become his dragon's home and put a tall rock in one corner so Captain Tim could bask under a heat lamp to get warm. He put a dragon-sized cave in another corner for Captain Tim to sleep in. Michael set up food and water bowls across from the cave, and he hung a little hammock near the heat lamp. When Michael first brought his bearded dragon home, he was just a little bigger than the lizards Michael used to catch in his grandparents' yard.

But Captain Tim grew and grew. And now he's almost two feet long from his nose to the tip of his tail.

Thankfully, he still fits in his tank—but Michael did have to buy him a bigger hammock!

Once a week, Michael takes Captain Tim out of his tank to let him stretch his legs. He always closes his door first to keep his dog, Sadie, out. Then he sets the orange dragon down on the floor so he can explore the room. Sometimes Captain Tim runs to Michael's desk and tries to climb up the wooden leg. Other times he runs to the tall window and basks in the sunlight. And every once in a while, the bearded dragon climbs onto Michael's bookcase and swats at all the books.

One day, Michael decided to give Captain Tim a really big adventure.

"Want to explore the house with me, Tim?" he asked, setting the dragon on his shoulder.

Captain Tim's claws dug into Michael's shirt. But Michael didn't mind. He just pretended he was a pirate and Captain Tim was his parrot-dragon. Michael walked Captain Tim down the stairs and around the family room, and he was heading to the laundry room when his dog, Sadie, came bounding through her doggy door. Sadie spotted the dragon on Michael's shoulder and barked.

Sadie got so excited, she started jumping on Michael.

"Sadie, no!" Michael shouted. "Sit!"

Sadie listened. But she kept wagging her tail, and she kept staring at Captain Tim.

"Sadie just wants to play," Michael told Captain Tim. "She's really loud and really big, but she wants to be your friend."

Michael told Sadie to stay, then slowly walked his dragon back upstairs and returned him to his glass tank. Just as Michael put the top back on, Sadie barked and scratched at his door.

Michael looked at Captain Tim. "She really is a good dog, but you should probably stick to having friends who couldn't accidentally eat you."

Captain Tim glanced up at Michael, bobbed his head, and then quickly scurried into his rock cave.

PAWS AND PONDER

What good advice did Michael give Captain Tim?
What good advice has someone given you? Has
   someone ever given you bad advice?
How can you tell the difference between good and
   bad advice?

Paws and Pray

Dear God, thank you for all the people you've put in my life who give me wise advice. Help me to be brave and ask them for help when I need it. And help me to give good advice to my friends when they need it.

Alfie and Peanut

When hope is crushed, the heart is crushed,
but a wish come true fills you with joy.

PROVERBS 13:12, GNT

LIKE MOST DOGS, Alfie loves to run after rabbits. But unlike most dogs, Alfie doesn't run after them to chase them away. The little dog runs after rabbits because he wants to be friends with them.

Every day, Alfie lies very still in his backyard and waits for a rabbit to hop out of the bushes. When one does, Alfie runs over to play.

But the bunnies get so scared when they see Alfie that they spin around and hop as fast as they can back to the bushes.

One day, Alfie thought he had finally found a rabbit who wanted to be friends. The small dog had been lying in the sun on the deck and was almost asleep when a little bunny hopped out from the bushes and started nibbling the grass near the deck steps. Alfie raced down the stairs but tripped on the last one. He tumbled off and landed on the rabbit! Alfie and the rabbit were so surprised to be touching each other that neither one of them moved for a minute. But then the rabbit shook his head, spun around, and dashed back to the bushes.

Months later, a group of people came to Alfie's house and started taking everything out and putting it in a truck. Alfie was confused. His human mom told him they were moving. She didn't look happy about it, so Alfie stayed close to her.

He also stayed close when they moved into a small apartment where everything smelled different. Alfie ran to the back door. There was no backyard, only a little balcony. How would he ever make friends with a rabbit if they didn't have a backyard?

Alfie's mom clipped his leash to his collar and said they were going for a walk. Alfie didn't want to go for a walk—he wanted to look for bunnies in his backyard. But he followed his mom out of their apartment and onto a walking trail. They hadn't gone very far when Alfie spotted another dog on a leash.

But then he realized it wasn't a dog.

It had tall ears, long back feet, and a little cotton-ball tail.

It was a rabbit!

Alfie couldn't believe his eyes. He ran over to the rabbit.

And the rabbit didn't run away!

"This is Peanut," Alfie heard the human say. "He loves going for walks."

Alfie sniffed Peanut.

Peanut sniffed Alfie.

And the two started hopping and jumping and playing.

A few days later, Alfie got to visit Peanut's apartment—which was right next door! They played with toys, they ate snacks, and they got so tired they took a nap together.

Alfie thought his dream of having a bunny friend would never come true, but now he has one for a best friend—and a next-door neighbor.

Why did none of the backyard rabbits want to be friends with Alfie?

How did Alfie's wish come true in an unexpected way?

Think of a time you really wanted something to happen—and it did! How did that make you feel?

Paws and Pray

Dear God, not getting something I want can be really hard. Please help me remember to trust you when I do get what I want—and when I don't. Help me to be patient and to believe that you will provide what I need.

Georgie

If you want to be happy, be kind to the
poor; it is a sin to despise anyone.

PROVERBS 14:21, GNT

KERI HAD WANTED a pet since she was really little.

"Sorry, sweetie," her mom would say, "but your dad
and I are allergic to animal fur. We can't have any
pets, or we would get sick."

Keri tried to understand, but it was hard. She really
wanted a pet.

One day when she walked outside, a grasshopper
jumped right in front of her. It was the biggest grasshopper she had ever seen.

She begged her mom to let her keep it.

"Um . . ." Her mom couldn't seem to find any other
words.

Keri took that as a yes and ran inside to find a
shoebox.

She finally had her very own pet!

She named him Georgie and made a cozy little bed for him in the corner of his shoebox. Her dad helped her cut a large hole out of the lid, cover it with clear plastic wrap, and poke holes in it so Georgie could get fresh air.

Keri could hardly wait to get to school the next day and tell her friends about her new pet. But they weren't very excited.

"Ew!" her friend Nikki said. "Grasshoppers are gross! They aren't pets—they're bugs you're supposed to squish!"

Keri's stomach did a flip-flop. She couldn't stand the thought of someone squishing Georgie.

"A grasshopper is a dumb pet," a boy named Adam said.

Keri felt sad. She wanted to cry—but not in front of Nikki and Adam.

When she got home, she took Georgie's box out on the back deck. She opened the lid and looked at her new friend.

Was a grasshopper a dumb pet?

Keri picked a leaf off one of her mom's plants and put it in Georgie's box.

She smiled when he started chewing on it. It didn't matter what Nikki and Adam thought. She liked Georgie and thought he was a great pet.

"You're not a dumb pet," she said, giving Georgie another leaf. "You're my friend—and the best pet for me."

Has anyone ever hurt your feelings? Have you ever
    hurt someone else's feelings?
How did Keri show kindness to Georgie?
How can you show kindness to someone today?

Paws and Pray

*Dear God, thank you for caring about me. Please help
me care about others and be kind to them—especially
people who are different from me and who like different
things than I do.*

Olivia's Happy

Whoever is patient has great understanding, but
one who is quick-tempered displays folly.

PROVERBS 14:29, NIV

OLIVIA COULDN'T HEAR very well when she
was a baby, which meant she had a hard time learning how to talk. When she was little, her words sounded
more like grunts and squeals. Most of the kids her age
couldn't understand her, and they would get frustrated
when they played with her.

But Olivia didn't mind, because she had Happy—
a big dog with an even bigger heart.

Happy didn't care that Olivia couldn't talk like
most of the other kids her age or that her ears didn't
work the way theirs did. He liked Olivia just the way
she was. And he was happiest when he was with her.

Olivia didn't know, or care, that to most people Happy
looked scary and intimidating. She liked him just the way
he was. And she was happiest when she was with *him*.

Happy always stayed close to Olivia, and he paid such close attention to her that over time he learned how to understand her.

He learned that when she pushed on his back, she wanted him to sit.

He learned that when she pushed on his side, she wanted him to lie down.

And he learned that when she made a squeaky, high-pitched sound, she wanted him to come to her.

Over time, Happy also learned how to play with Olivia.

He learned to sit still for tea parties and how to drink from tiny cups.

He learned how to roll on his back and let her give him a checkup whenever she brought out her doctor's kit.

And he learned how to give her stuffed animals a ride when she put them in an empty laundry basket and tied a scarf from the basket to his collar.

Happy and Olivia spent every day together, and they learned how to make each other feel loved.

Even when Olivia learned how to speak and communicate with others, Happy was still her best friend. He could understand what she needed, and she could always talk to him—even when she didn't want to use words.

He was always her Happy, and she was always his favorite girl.

How did Happy show patience to Olivia? How did
   his patience help her?

Why is it important to be patient with others?

How can you show patience to a family member or
   friend?

Paws and Pray

*Dear God, sometimes it's hard for me to be patient.
Please help me to be understanding with others, especially with those who are different from me. And thank
you for always being so patient with me.*

Sunny's Hedgehog

A peaceful heart leads to a healthy body;
jealousy is like cancer in the bones.

PROVERBS 14:30

MARCUS KICKED HIS soccer ball as hard as he could. His mom had promised to play soccer with him, but his baby sister, Bree, started crying, and his mom went to check on her. It seemed like all his sister could do was cry. Marcus kicked the ball again.

All his friends were away on summer vacations. But he was stuck at home with a new baby. Marcus didn't want to play by himself, so he went back inside. He saw his mom holding Bree in her arms. His dog, Sunny, ran to him. She was carrying a hedgehog stuffed animal in her mouth.

"I'm sorry, buddy," his mom said. "Bree got really hungry and needs to eat. We can play as soon as she's done."

"Okay," Marcus mumbled. But it didn't feel okay. He wanted to play now. Marcus sat beside Sunny. She put her head in his lap and sighed. He ran his fingers through Sunny's long fur.

After Bree finished eating, she let out a big burp. Marcus laughed—even though he still felt mad. He hadn't expected such a loud sound to come from such a tiny person. His mom laughed too and then put Bree in the baby swing. She buckled her in and pushed the buttons to turn on the swing. A few minutes later, Sunny put her hedgehog on the floor next to the swing.

"What is she doing?" Marcus asked.

"I think she's pretending her hedgehog is her baby," his mom answered. "She did the same thing when we brought you home from the hospital. The vet said dogs do that sometimes when they are adjusting to a new baby in the house."

Would a dog really know to do that? Marcus wondered. *Maybe Sunny accidentally dropped her hedgehog next to the swing.*

But later that night, when Marcus's mom gave Bree a bath and Sunny plopped her hedgehog in the bathtub, he knew that Sunny really was pretending to take care of her own baby.

"You're a funny dog," Marcus said, taking the wet stuffed animal out of the water.

When Marcus leaned over, Bree's tiny hand smacked the water and splashed his face.

"Hey!" Marcus laughed. He put his finger near Bree's hand and felt happy when she grabbed it.

After bathtime, Marcus's mom asked if he would like to pick out a book to read to Bree. That made him happy too. He ran to his room and got his favorite—one about dinosaurs. Marcus held the book so his baby sister—and Sunny's hedgehog—could see the pictures.

Marcus might not have been able to play soccer with his mom that day, and he knew things were going to be different, but he was glad to have a sister. He realized he really liked being a big brother to his baby sister—and to Sunny's hedgehog.

PAWS AND PONDER

Why did Marcus feel jealous?

When have you been jealous? What does being jealous feel like?

What do you think helped Marcus change his mind about his baby sister?

Paws and Pray

Dear God, when I start to feel jealous, please help me remember how much you love me and how much you have done for me. And if my jealous feelings start to feel too big, please help me be brave enough to talk to someone I trust and ask them for help.

Good Night, Jade

When people are happy, they smile, but when they are sad, they look depressed.

PROVERBS 15:13, GNT

DREW'S MOM HAD TEARS in her eyes when she walked into his room. He knew what she was going to say, but he didn't want to hear it, so he kept playing with his Legos.

"Jade died at the vet's this morning, sweetheart," his mom said. "The doctor said that her body was too old and sick to fight the cancer anymore."

His mom put her hand on his back and gave a little squeeze. Usually, he liked when she did that. It made him feel safe. But right now, it made him feel mad. Drew leaned away from her.

"It's okay to cry," his mom said, wiping tears from her eyes. "I know you loved Jade very much."

And he did. Jade was four years old when Drew was born—he had loved her his whole life.

How could she be gone? Nothing his mom was saying felt real.

Drew's throat felt tight, but he was too sad to cry.

Too mad to yell.

And too confused to ask questions.

He just wanted to be alone to finish his Lego set.

Later that day when his dad got home, they planted a small tree in the backyard in memory of Jade. But Drew didn't want a tree—he wanted his dog.

He wanted his dog when he came home from school and the house was quiet.

He wanted his dog for show-and-tell when other kids brought in pictures of their pets.

And he wanted his dog when he got sick and couldn't fall asleep.

Sometimes when Drew played outside with his friends, he would forget about being sad and missing Jade. But when nighttime came and Jade didn't jump up on his bed with him, all the sad, mad, and confused feelings would come back.

One night, when Drew's mom came to tuck him in, she handed him a stuffed animal. It looked like Jade.

"I know you're probably too old for stuffed animals now, but I saw this today and thought maybe your bed missed having a dog on it."

Drew hugged his mom.

"I miss Jade," he whispered, holding the stuffed dog close.

"Me too," his mom whispered back.

When his mom left, Drew set the stuffed animal on the part of his bed where Jade always lay. It wasn't the same. But it helped a little.

"Good night, Jade. I love you."

Has a pet or someone you loved died? What were
    some of the feelings you felt when that happened?
Was there anything that helped you feel better?
How could you help someone who has big feelings
    about something sad?

Paws and Pray

*Dear God, it's so hard when people and animals we love
die. It's hard to feel such big—and sometimes scary—
feelings. Please help me to remember that you are
always with me. And help me remember I can always
talk to you about my feelings and ask you to help me.*

Forgiving Lucky

A hot-tempered person stirs up conflict, but
the one who is patient calms a quarrel.

PROVERBS 15:18, NIV

EMMA LOVED CATS. She wished she could have a cat of her own, but her dog, Tonka, didn't like cats.

Thankfully, Emma's Aunt Jackie loved cats too—and she didn't have a dog.

Aunt Jackie fostered cats—she took care of cats who needed a home until she could find someone to adopt them.

She called Emma to tell her she had three kittens in her house and then asked if Emma would like to help her take care of them.

Emma was so excited. The kittens—Cleo, Bella, and Lucky—were really cute. She loved all of them, but Lucky was her favorite. His gray-and-white-striped coat was so soft, and he liked being held like a baby.

At first, Emma had been scared to pick him up. She had never held a kitten before. But Aunt Jackie showed her where to put her hands, and as soon as Emma picked him up, Lucky snuggled into her arms and purred.

Every time Emma visited, Lucky tried to climb up her leg and get into her arms. As Lucky grew, he got a little heavier, but not too heavy for Emma to hold. And she was glad. She loved holding Lucky.

One day, when Emma was standing in the kitchen talking to Aunt Jackie, Lucky started trying to climb her leg. Emma laughed and scooped him up. Lucky purred and snuggled into her arms. But when Cleo and Bella ran into the kitchen, Lucky sat up and smacked Emma in the face with his little paw. His claw scratched her lip. She was so surprised—and confused. Lucky jumped out of her arms. Emma tried not to cry, but her lip hurt.

Her heart hurt more.

Aunt Jackie ran to get ice and some ointment for Emma's lip.

"I am so sorry. I don't know what got into him," Aunt Jackie said, helping Emma put ice on her lip.

Emma just wanted to go home. *Why did Lucky scratch me? What did I do wrong?*

The next time Emma went to visit, she didn't pick Lucky up—even when he tried to climb her leg. She missed holding him, but she didn't want him to scratch her again.

After a while, Aunt Jackie realized that Lucky would hit or scratch when he wanted down. She started working with him to help him learn better manners.

Several weeks after first getting scratched, Emma visited Aunt Jackie again. Lucky started meowing loudly and tried to climb up Emma's leg.

Emma had forgiven Lucky for scratching her, but she still wasn't quite ready to trust that he wouldn't scratch her again. So Emma sat down beside the kitten and patted her knees. Lucky climbed up, snuggled onto her lap, and began to purr.

It wasn't quite the same as before, but Emma was happy to have her Lucky back. And she knew in time she would learn to trust him again.

Why do you think Emma was scared to hold Lucky again after he scratched her?

What does it mean to forgive someone?

Have you ever had to forgive someone? What was the hardest part about forgiving them?

Paws and Pray

Dear God, thank you for forgiving me when I mess up. Please help me to forgive others when they hurt my feelings. And please help me to be brave and ask for forgiveness when I hurt other people.

Buddy the Frog

Smiling faces make you happy, and good
news makes you feel better.

PROVERBS 15:30, GNT

ANDY DIDN'T WANT to leave his grandparents'
house. Staying with them was his favorite part of his
family's summer vacation. He loved waking up early
to get donuts with his granddad, playing with his
grandma's old typewriter, and watching the sunset at
the beach. And he really loved sitting on their back
porch at night, listening to the green tree frogs call out
to each other.

"Why do we have to leave tomorrow?" Andy asked
his mom after dinner.

"Because your dad and I have to get back to work,
and you have to start school," she answered.

Andy liked his house and his school, but he wished

he lived closer to his grandparents. Three hundred miles was a really long way.

Andy walked out to the porch to find his granddad. He wished he could climb up on his lap like he used to when he was little. His granddad patted the swing beside him, and Andy hurried to sit down.

"I wish we lived closer," Granddad said.

"Me too," Andy whispered.

They rocked back and forth on the swing for a little while. Then they heard a tree frog call out.

This one sounded close—much closer than the others they were used to hearing far out in the trees.

Andy's granddad stood up. Andy followed him to the corner of the screened porch.

A green tree frog was clinging to the top of the screen!

"What do we do?" Andy asked.

"You stay here and keep an eye on him. I'll be right back."

Andy stared at the frog until his granddad came back, holding an empty plastic food container and the spatula his grandma used to make pancakes. Andy didn't think Grandma would be too happy about that.

Granddad held the open container under the tree frog and scooted the frog into it with the spatula. He put the lid on the container. Andy noticed there were several little holes in the lid so the frog could get air.

"I think maybe this little guy was trying to tell us that he would like to go home with you," Granddad said.

Andy looked at the bright-green frog and smiled. His old glass fish tank would make a great home for this frog. Andy had been reading all about tree frogs and knew how to take care of one. He threw his arms around his granddad.

He still wished he could stay—or that his grandparents could live closer—but his new tree frog made things feel a little bit better.

And every night when Buddy, his tree frog, starts to make his tree frog sounds, Andy smiles and thinks about his granddad—who is thinking about him too.

Why do you think Andy's granddad gave him the
   tree frog?
Why did the frog help Andy feel better?
What helps you feel better when you're sad?

Paws and Pray

*Dear God, thank you for all the ways you help me—and
for being with me, even when I'm sad. I am so glad I
never have to say goodbye to you, because I know you're
always here.*

A Daisy for Imani

We may make our plans, but God has the last word.

PROVERBS 16:1, GNT

IMANI HAD BEEN so happy at the beginning of the school year. She really liked her teachers and had made some good friends. She was even starting to like math and spelling better. And she was excited to sing a solo at the spring concert.

But the night after Imani's first concert practice, her mom told her that all the schools in their city had to close because of a pandemic that was making people sick. Her school was going to move online, but they wouldn't get to do the concert.

Imani didn't want people to get sick, but she was sad to miss her concert—and her first solo.

Imani started to feel happy again when online school started. It was fun to go to school in her pajamas and to see her friends' pets. And her teacher tried

to make their lessons fun by wearing costumes and doing funny voices. But after a few days, Imani missed being with her friends. She missed playing with them at recess and sitting with them at lunch. She also started having trouble paying attention during her lessons. And math and spelling felt hard again.

"I miss my friends," Imani told her mom one night at bedtime.

"Me too," her mom said.

Imani thought her mom's eyes looked sad. *Maybe everyone feels a little sad right now*, she thought.

A few weeks after online school started, Imani's mom walked into her room. She was holding a towel. And the towel was . . . wiggling. Imani walked over to get a better look.

It was a kitten!

"Where did you get a kitten?" Imani squealed.

"One of our neighbor's cats had kittens a little while ago, and this one needs a home. What do you think? Should we give her a home here?"

Imani nodded her head so fast she made herself dizzy.

She and her mom decided that the orange-and-white cat looked like a Daisy, so that's what they named her. Imani made a little bed for Daisy in her room. Her mom set up a litter box and food and water bowls in the laundry room. And they made cat toys out of sticks, yarn, and pretend feathers they found in an old craft bin.

Imani loved playing with Daisy. She made their house feel a little happier. And she gave Imani and her mom something to think about besides all the things they missed doing. Imani also liked holding Daisy on her lap while she did online school.

It wasn't the same as playing tag with her friends at recess or sharing their lunches in the cafeteria, but Daisy was a good friend.

And the little cat helped Imani and her mom find their smiles again.

PAWS AND PONDER

What were some of Imani's plans at the beginning of the story? How did they change?

Have you ever had plans change? How did that make you feel?

How do you think God helped Imani and her mom? How has God helped you when your plans had to change?

Paws and Pray

Dear God, thank you for always being there and for never changing. Our plans don't always stay the same, but you do. Help me to trust you, even when I feel disappointed.

A Big Job for Levi

Commit your work to the LORD, and
your plans will be established.

PROVERBS 16:3, ESV

LEVI IS A SMALL DOG with a very big job—he helps people feel better.

When Levi was a puppy, not much bigger than the squirrels he likes to chase, his human mom, Heidi, knew he was special.

"You always make my heart so happy," Heidi told him. "And I know you can help other people feel happy too. You can help them feel God's love."

Heidi took Levi to dog school, where he learned what different words mean—like *sit*, *stay*, *lie down*, and *wait*. Levi learned those words and commands very quickly, and he liked practicing them at home with Heidi.

One day, Heidi put a blue vest on him. Levi felt important in his vest. He sat up straight and looked at Heidi to find out what they were going to do.

"This vest tells people that you are a very special dog called a therapy dog," Heidi told him. "Your vest is like your uniform."

Levi didn't know what a uniform was, but he liked wearing his vest. He *really* liked going for car rides. And he *really, really* liked when Heidi took him into a big building and let him visit lots of kids. The kids looked like they didn't feel very good. Some of them had tubes connected to their arms. Some didn't have any hair. And some couldn't get out of bed. But Levi didn't mind any of that. He was just happy to make new friends.

Levi liked snuggling beside a girl while she petted his light-brown fur.

He liked chasing after a ball that a boy rolled down the hallway.

And he really liked when some kids read their favorite book to him.

"You're such a good therapy dog," Heidi told Levi.

Levi wagged his little tail. He didn't know what a therapy dog was, but he was happy that Heidi was happy. And Levi loved making so many friends.

Levi likes helping kids feel brave.

He likes being their friend.

And he really likes making them smile.

Levi is glad Heidi took him to dog school and bought him a blue vest. But most of all, he is happy when he helps kids feel better. Because to Levi, that's the best job of all.

PAWS AND PONDER

Have you ever met a therapy dog?
Why do you think so many people like dogs?
What is something you can do today to help
someone feel God's love?

Paws and Pray

*Dear God, thank you for giving us animals that help us
see and feel your love. Please help me show your love to
others. And please help those who are sick, lonely, or sad
to feel your love today.*

About the Author

JENNIFER MARSHALL BLEAKLEY is also the author of *Joey: How a Blind Rescue Horse Helped Others Learn to See* and *Project Solomon: The True Story of a Lonely Horse Who Found a Home—and Became a Hero*, as well as the Pawverbs devotional series. She has worked as a child and family grief counselor and holds a master's degree in mental health counseling from Nova Southeastern University. She lives in Raleigh, North Carolina, with her husband, Darrell, their two children, and a menagerie of animals. You can connect with Jen online at jenniferbleakley.com or on social media @jenbleakley.

Acknowledgments

WRITING A BOOK IS a big job that takes a lot of time and hard work, but it is also really, really fun. One of the most fun things about writing this book was thinking about you reading it! Every time I would sit down to write a story, I would imagine a kid—just like you—opening it, and that would make me smile. Then I would pet my dog, Gracie, and my cat, Foxy—who both like to sit beside me while I type on my computer—and I would start to write a story, just for you.

So thank *you* for making this such a special book! I hope you like reading it as much as I liked writing it.

I also want to say a big thank you to some other special people who helped make this book:

Sarah Atkinson, thank you for having the vision for Pawverbs as a devotional series. You are such a blessing.

Linda Howard, thank you for inviting me into the Tyndale Kids family. This book is a dream come true for me, as is working with you!

Danika Kelly, it has been a joy to work with you! Thank you for all of your work on this book. You are so talented, and this book is so much better because of you.

Ron Kaufmann, I can't imagine Pawverbs without you! Thank you so much for creating such gorgeous and special books. These books would not be what they are without you.

A big thank you to Karen McGraw, Michelle Polsley, and Claire Lloyd. I am so honored to get to work with such an amazing (and downright PAWsome) team!

I also want to thank my friends Sarah and Carol for sending me funny texts and making me laugh while I worked on this book, and Aimee, Julie, Brooklyn, Tracy, Jodi G., Jodi S., and Barbara for giving me story ideas and always being there for me.

I want to say a big thank you to my mom and dad for loving me, praying for me, and helping me remember my own animal stories from when I was a kid.

Aunt Judy, thank you for believing that I can do anything and for always being there.

Darrell, you are my safe place and my home. I couldn't do this without your support.

Andrew and Ella, never forget that Pawverbs started with you! Andrew, thank you for introducing the Paws family into our lives. It's so amazing to think how God was planting the seeds for these books all the way back then. Thank you both for letting me make up Pawverbs stories that summer when I forgot to pack your bedtime books. What I thought was a disaster, God used to make something really great.

I started writing for you, and you will always be a part of everything I do.

And God, thank you for giving us such wonderful animals that help us learn things about you. Thank you for letting me write these stories, and thank you for loving me. Please let all my friends reading this book know that you love them and that you think they are really, really special.

Photography Credits

Unless otherwise noted, interior photographs are from Depositphotos and are the property of their respective copyright holders, and all rights are reserved. Listed by page number:

For all ages: more *heartwarming* tales of real-life pets by Jennifer Marshall Bleakley

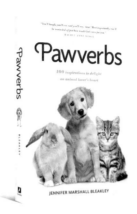

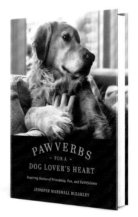

Available wherever books are sold.